QUINOA

QUINOA
A BOOK OF RECIPES

PENNY DOYLE

LORENZ BOOKS

First published in 2014 by Lorenz Books
an imprint of Anness Publishing Limited
108 Great Russell Street, London WC1B 3NA
www.annesspublishing.com
www.lorenzbooks.com; info@anness.com

If you like the images in this book and would like to investigate
using them for publishing, promotions or advertising, please visit
our website www.practicalpictures.com for more information

A CIP catalogue record for this book is available from
The British Library

Publisher Joanna Lorenz
Editorial Director Helen Sudell
Editor: Joanne Rippin
Photographer: Nicki Dowey
Food Stylists: Lucy McKelvie, Jayne Cross, Emma Jane Frost
Props Stylist: Lucy Harvey
Designer Nigel Partridge
Illustrations Anna Koska

This book was previously published as part of a larger volume,
The Quinoa Cookbook

Printed and bound in China

COOK'S NOTES

· Bracketed terms are intended for American readers.

· For all recipes, quantities are given in both metric and imperial
measures and, where appropriate, in standard cups and spoons.
Follow one set of measures, but not a mixture, because they are not
interchangeable.

· Standard spoon and cup measures are level. 1 tsp = 5ml,
1 tbsp = 15ml, 1 cup = 250ml/8fl oz.

· Australian standard tablespoons are 20ml. Australian readers
should use 3 tsp in place of 1 tbsp for measuring small quantities.

· American pints are 16fl oz/2 cups. American readers should use
20fl oz/2.5 cups in place of 1 pint when measuring liquids.

· Electric oven temperatures in this book are for conventional ovens.
When using a fan oven, the temperature will probably need to be
reduced by about 10–20°C/20–40°F. Since ovens vary, you should
check with your manufacturer's instruction book for guidance.

· The nutritional analysis given for each recipe is calculated per
portion (i.e. serving or item), unless otherwise stated. If the recipe
gives a range, such as Serves 4–6, then the nutritional analysis will
be for the smaller portion size, i.e. 6 servings. The analysis does not
include optional ingredients, such as salt added to taste.

· Medium (US large) eggs are used unless otherwise stated.

GLUTEN-FREE

Recipes listed as gluten-free contain no naturally gluten-containing
ingredients et wheat, rye or barley. However, many manufactured
foods eg stock cubes, some yogurts and soy sauce, may contain
gluten, so you will need to refer to National Coeliac/Celiac
guidelines etc Coeliac UK or Celiac Disease Foundation (US) to
ensure that you have suitable gluten-free brands where necessary.

PUBLISHER'S NOTE

CONTENTS

INTRODUCTION 6

TYPES OF QUINOA 8

HEALTH PROPERTIES OF QUINOA 10

COOKING WITH QUINOA 12

BE CREATIVE WITH QUINOA 14

BREAKFASTS AND LIGHT MEALS 16

FISH AND MEAT MAINS 34

VEGETARIAN MAINS 44

DESSERTS AND BAKES 54

INDEX 64

INTRODUCTION

Quinoa's rise from a unique dietary staple of the South Americans to its status as an emerging Western 'superfood' is quite remarkable. The nutritional superiority of quinoa (pronounced 'keen-wa') is driving international demand, and productivity has increased by over a third in recent years. Comparable to other starchy staples such as rice or potato, quinoa boasts more protein,

Below: Use quinoa flakes in granola, flapjacks and crumbles.

healthy fats, calcium, iron and B vitamins than any other food. It is also cholesterol and gluten-free, and has the added benefit of being wholegrain.

In modern kitchens as well as prestigious restaurants around the world, chefs and home cooks are discovering the versatility of quinoa in all its forms, while health-conscious athletes and dieticians are becoming converted to its nutritional benefits.

Whether used as a grain, rolled, as flour, puffed or as pasta, quinoa is proving a welcome change to the carbohydrate staples of pasta, rice, potatoes and couscous.

The quinoa we buy today is the seed of the plant *Chenopodium quino*. It is classified by some nutritionists as a 'pseudograin' because it contains a similar nutritional profile and cooking properties to other grains, though technically it is actually a seed.

Above: A head of seeds on the quinoa plant.

FOOD OF THE INCAS

Native to the Altiplano people of South America, who started cultivating it over 6,000 years ago, quinoa was an esteemed food of the Incas who used it as a staple cereal in beer and bread. It was considered such a valuable part of the diet in areas of the Andean mountains, where agriculture was challenged by altitude and temperatures, that it was more precious than gold, and many believed it had spiritual properties. The Incas referred to it as *la chisiya mama* (the mother grain), as they thought it also gave longevity.

Quinoa was particularly valued as food for Inca warriors, who had to travel around the large Incan Empire by marching for weeks at high altitudes, without access to meat or vegetation. Quinoa provided crucial stamina and endurance, and the warriors would often eat it mixed with fat in the form of 'warballs'.

Recognizing its power, quinoa was unsuccessfully targeted for destruction by the Spanish Conquistadors during their invasion in 1500s, when cultivating it was deemed a crime that was punishable by death. The survival of cultivated quinoa was testament to the bravery and ingenuity of the indigenous peoples, who secretly tended plantations high in the Andes, where quinoa evolved to survive harsh climates of drought, frost and intense sunlight, able to grow in

Above: The seeds of the quinoa plant have to be milled and washed thoroughly before they are sold at market.

temperatures between 18–100°F/-8–38°C. Having proved its enduring resilience during this period, quinoa earned its 'supergrain' status and today enjoys international cultivation. So far, however, growers in other regions, including Canada, Colorado, Europe and Kenya are unable to match the quality of the excellent, light coloured, sweetly delicate seed that comes from the high mountains of South America.

USING THIS BOOK

This collection of 25 inspiring recipes brings vibrant tastes and flavour combinations from around the world to create tempting and delicious dishes, which are full of superfood nutrition. There are plenty of tips to help you get the most from this valuable food and ideas for variations. The book will help you maximize your use of quinoa, and impress those who have yet to discover the Inca's 'mother of all grains'.

TYPES OF QUINOA

Quinoa is available in a few different forms, which makes its use in the kitchen much more versatile. Large supermarkets more and more frequently stock pearl quinoa, but you can also find red and black quinoa online or at health stores, as well as quinoa flakes, pasta, quinoa pops and flour.

PEARL QUINOA
The creamy white grains of pearl quinoa are the most widely available type. It can be used in savoury dishes instead of other carbohydrates, in salads either as a cooked grain or sprouted, and in breakfast cereals and desserts. It has a

light and fluffy texture when cooked, with a nutty flavour.

RED QUINOA
This is usually less frequently available and more expensive. It can be used in the same way as pearl quinoa but has a vibrant orange-brown colour, a slightly firmer texture and a nuttier flavour when cooked. It is wonderful mixed with different coloured quinoa.

BLACK QUINOA
This is the firmest of the quinoa seeds, having almost a 'crunch' even when cooked. Use as for pearl or red quinoa, or mix them for a vibrant visual effect.

TRICOLOUR QUINOA
This a commercial mix usually of red, black and pearl quinoa, which makes very pretty dishes, particularly in salads and sprinkled over stir-fries. The black quinoa usually means the cooked result retains some 'bite', which helps create a contrast of texture. You can, of course, mix your own.

QUINOA FLOUR

A textured, gluten-free flour that is available from health stores or online. It is easy to make yourself by grinding raw quinoa in a food processor. Quinoa flour is used as a thickener in sauces, in baking breads, cakes, cookies and pastry, and even in some baked desserts. Quinoa flour is best stored in the refrigerator for freshness.

QUINOA FLAKES

These flakes are quinoa seeds that have been rolled, a similar process to porridge oats, and used in the same way. Substitute quinoa flakes for oats in porridge, muesli, granola, crumbles or baking. They retain a slightly firmer texture than oats when cooked.

QUINOA PASTA

This pasta may be made entirely with quinoa flour, or a mixture of quinoa and rice flours. It is cooked in the same way as regular pasta, and tastes very similar. It can be sourced locally or through online suppliers and is a simple way of adding quinoa to a family's diet with very little effort.

QUINOA SPROUTS

These are sprouted quinoa seeds made by storing soaked quinoa in a dark place for a few hours, and are a way of adding extra crunch and nutrients to salads and sandwiches.

QUINOA POPS

These are puffed quinoa seeds that look like much smaller puffed wheat. They are available from online suppliers.

HEALTHY PROPERTIES OF QUINOA

The term 'superfood' is justifiably used to describe quinoa, as it can boast an incredible nutritional profile compared to other grains and carbohydrates. Quinoa is also easy to store, transport and cook, and is inexpensive.

NUTRIENT PROFILE
Quinoa has hugely impressive health benefits, first realized by the Incas, but now backed up and proven by modern analysis and research. Granted the

Below: Quinoa flour is a healthier way of baking.

nutrient status of 'esteemed' and containing a protein content varying between 12 and 20 percent, quinoa contains all nine essential amino acids (the protein building-blocks) including rarer lysine, methionine, cystine and histidine. The latter is considered essential in the development of children, and is believed to help promote healthy pregnancies and enhance breast milk.

On the basis of its amino acid profile alone, quinoa is considered superior to wheat, barley or even the soya bean. Quinoa is universally favoured by athletes, and those in power sports such as body building, as it helps restore and build muscle after training. It is also low in fat, cholesterol-free, and a good source of fibre, B vitamins and minerals including iron, calcium, copper, manganese, magnesium, chloride and potassium.

Above: Tricolour quinoa adds vibrancy as well as texture.

Some research claims that quinoa has medical as well as nutritional benefits. It is possible that quinoa is a useful food for headache sufferers as the magnesium may help blood flow in the brain, therefore easing pain. Quinoa's rich natural antioxidants, which act as a natural preservative of the grain, may help lower the risk of some cancers. There is also growing interest among the medical community in its possible anti-inflammatory properties that may help rheumatoid arthritis sufferers.

GLUTEN-FREE

Unlike many grains eg wheat, barley or rye, quinoa doesn't contain gluten, which can cause gut problems and malabsorption in those diagnosed with coeliac disease. It is therefore a valuable alternative to pasta, cereals and bread for coeliacs, but also for the growing number of people who are gluten-intolerant, and feel better on gluten-free diets.

WHOLEGRAIN

Quinoa is also termed a 'wholegrain' since it contains all three elements of a seed (germ, endosperm and bran). Eating more wholegrains is associated with a lower risk of chronic diseases including heart disease, diabetes and some cancers. Partly because of its wholegrain status, quinoa is also a low Glycaemic Index (GI) food. GI relates to how quickly carbohydrate foods raise your blood sugar levels and how full you may feel after eating them. Low GI foods like quinoa, sweet

Above: Add sprouted quinoa to salad for a nutritious lunch.

potato and granary bread keep you feeling fuller for longer than higher GI foods such as potato and white bread.

HIGH FIBRE

Fibre is essential to the health and functioning of our digestive systems, and can be soluble or insoluble. Quinoa is a high-fibre food with the dual benefits of both soluble (one third) and insoluble fibre (two thirds). Soluble fibre keeps cholesterol levels lower by helping to block its absorption from food. It may also help lower blood pressure

and other unhealthy fats in our blood. Insoluble fibre is undigested by the gut and vital for preventing constipation, haemorrhoids, and gut-related diseases including cancer. Fibre-rich foods also help improve the sensitivity of insulin, which may lower the incidences of Type II diabetes.

As a fibre-rich food alone, quinoa has significant health benefits, but when this is added to its other amazing nutritional attributes, it is clear that this wonderful grain really does qualify as a superfood.

Below: Quinoa flakes and dried fruits make a fabulous muesli.

COOKING WITH QUINOA

The small size of this 'pseudo grain' means it takes less time to cook than other comparable grains and makes nearly three times its volume after absorbing cooking liquid. Quinoa should be 'al dente' with a little bit of bite, but cooking time can of course be adjusted to suit the dish it is to be used in.

REMOVING SAPONINS

Quinoa needs rinsing in water before cooking, to remove natural 'saponins' that coat the seed. Saponins contribute to the hardiness of quinoa as they act as natural pesticides during cultivation.

Unfortunately saponins have a bitter taste, but this can easily be removed by rinsing. Most commercial quinoa is already rinsed, but it's likely some saponins will remain. Running water through quinoa in a sieve or colander, and rubbing it with your fingers, will remove any residues. Once rinsed, there are several ways that you can cook quinoa.

Simmer and absorb: Rinse the quinoa in water. Add 1 part quinoa to 2 parts water in a pan. Bring to the boil, cover and simmer for 14–16 minutes until all of the water is absorbed. There is no need to stir.

Set aside the quinoa in the pan, covered and off the heat, for up to a further 10 minutes if a plumper texture is required. Little water should remain, but drain off any excess.

Boil and drain: This is a good method for removing excess saponins. Rinse the quinoa and

STORING QUINOA

Its high polyunsaturated fat content means quinoa degrades quickly unless stored in a cool place. This means a dark cupboard, in an airtight container. Keep quinoa flour in an airtight container in the refrigerator. Store quinoa 'pops' in an airtight container. Cooked quinoa should be kept in the refrigerator, covered, and used within a week. It can also be frozen and stored in plastic bags, and kept in the freezer to use as needed.

add to a large pan of boiling water (1 part quinoa to 4 parts water approximately).

Bring to the boil and simmer, uncovered, for about 15 minutes until the quinoa is plump and fluffy, then drain and serve.

Steaming: Rinse the quinoa. Follow the manufacturer's

instructions for cooking white rice in an electric, hob or microwave steamer, but remember that quinoa will expand to twice its uncooked volume, so allow space for this.

Slow cooking: Rinse the quinoa, and follow the manufacturer's instructions for cooking white rice.

Or add quinoa to soups and casseroles, using 1 part quinoa to 2 parts stock. Serve soon after cooking to prevent the quinoa absorbing the stock.

Baking: Place the quinoa with stock or water (1 part quinoa to 2 parts water/stock) in a

casserole dish, cover and bake in the oven at 350°F/180°C/ Gas 4 for 30–35 minutes.

Dry roasting: Rinse and pat dry the quinoa. Spread it on a large, ungreased baking sheet Bake at 180°C/350°F/Gas 4 for 25–35 minutes until golden and crunchy. Cool then store in an airtight container. Use in granola, or as a salad topping.

USING COOKED QUINOA

The table below will help you to calculate how to cook the correct amount of quinoa for the recipes in this book, some of which use cooked quinoa as a starting point.

Remember if you are using more concentrated fluids to cook quinoa, such as milk or fruit juice in puddings or porridges, higher volumes of fluid will be needed to help the quinoa cook until tender. As a rule of thumb add an extra 25%, for example 1 part quinoa to 2.5 parts milk/fruit juice/syrup, but be ready to add a little more during the cooking process.

COOKING QUANTITIES

This table shows you how to achieve the required yield of cooked quinoa used in some recipes. As a rule of thumb: 1 part quinoa + 2 parts water/stock = 3 parts cooked quinoa. Note: 1 cup raw quinoa = 190g = 6½oz; 1 cup cooked quinoa = 165g = 5½oz.

Raw Quinoa	Water	Cooked Quinoa Yield
40g/1½oz/¼ cup	125ml/4fl oz/½ cup	125g/4½oz/¾ cup
50g/2oz/⅓ cup	160ml/5fl oz/⅔ cup	165g/5½oz/1 cup
75g/3oz/½ cup	250ml/8fl oz/1 cup	275g/10oz/1½ cups
95g/3.½oz/⅔ cup	320ml/11fl oz/1⅓ cup	375g/13oz/2 cups
115g/4oz/¾ cup	360ml/12fl oz/1½ cups	440g/15½oz/2¼ cups
190g/6½oz/1 cup	500ml/16fl oz/2 cups	560g/1lb 4oz/3 cups

BE CREATIVE WITH QUINOA

Quinoa can be incorporated into many classic dishes adding colour, texture and flavour that give the recipes a new dimension. The following guidelines will give you ideas for including quinoa in your favourite everyday recipes and benefiting from quinoa's impressive nutrient 'punch'.

BREAD
You can substitute quinoa flour for regular 'strong' bread flour in your favourite recipes, but

Below: Quinoa flour makes wonderfully nutty breads.

remember that as it is gluten-free, the strength of the dough and therefore its ability to rise will be reduced. Substituting only up to half the amount of strong bread flour will help to produce a lighter loaf.

You can use both quinoa flour and cooked pearl quinoa in pizza dough, which is a fantastic way to boost the nutrient content of an everyday family favourite. Substitute up to a half of the regular wheat flour with quinoa flour, but remember the gluten content of the dough will be lower so you will get a thinner and crispier result rather than a 'deep pan' base.

PASTRY
Quinoa's essential fats ensure a delicious, light-textured pastry that can be used for quiches and sweet and savoury pies. Make pastry using the usual ratio of half fat to flour, but substitute half the flour with

Above: Quinoa flour in baking gives a very crisp result, and is perfect for making cookies.

quinoa flour, or quinoa flakes for a more coarse texture. Because of its higher fat content and lack of gluten, the end result will be crisp, but the pastry can be very 'short' and crumbly to work with, so needs to be rested in the refrigerator for at least 30 minutes.

BAKING
Substitute the same weight of quinoa flakes for rolled oats, or quinoa flour for regular flour in your favourite recipes, but

Above: Red and black quinoa's dramatic colour is a vibrant addition to salads.

add a little more vanilla extract or other flavouring to be sure that the quinoa doesn't dominate. If using quinoa pops instead of flakes, remember to halve the weight to take account of the quinoa pops' low density.

RICE DISHES

Quinoa can be substituted for any type of rice to make delicious, risottos, paellas or pilaffs with bite and texture. To adapt your favourite rice recipe use quinoa in the same way you would use basmati or arborio rice, softening it first in butter and then adding the correct quantity of stock, together with meat, fish or vegetables. Simmer on a gentle heat, uncovered, for 8–10 minutes, until all the liquid has been absorbed. Stirring constantly for a risotto isn't necessary when using quinoa.

SALADS

Using different coloured quinoa will give you striking salads that can be complemented by adding an array of different grains, vegetables, fruit, nuts and seeds.

Incorporate quinoa sprouts for added crunch and texture. Use intensely flavoured dressings of oil, vinegar, fresh herbs, mustard and soy sauce.

STUFFINGS

Cooked quinoa is useful in stuffings instead of breadcrumbs and will absorb the rich flavours of any meat or fish that it is cooked with. It is also great in stuffed vegetables.

CRISPY COATINGS

Cooked, fluffed pearl quinoa is an effective alternative to breadcrumbs as a gluten-free substitute, and can be used for crispy fried fish, chicken or vegetables. Wash and pat dry the food and dust with flour, then dip into beaten egg. Coat in seasoned cooked pearl quinoa and shallow-fry in oil until golden, turning occasionally. Around 150g/5oz/1 cup of cooked quinoa will coat 3–4 medium fish fillets, or 2 chicken breasts cut into goujons.

Below: Quinoa is a nutritious substitute for rice in risottos, pilaffs and paellas.

BREAKFASTS AND LIGHT MEALS

QUINOA CONTAINS SOLUBLE FIBRE THAT IS

IDEAL FOR A SUSTAINING MEAL, WHICH WILL

KEEP YOU SATISFIED FOR LONGER. START THE

DAY WITH A DELICIOUS BOWL OF MUESLI, ENJOY

A STACK OF QUINOA PANCAKES OR SHARE A

REFRESHING SALAD AT LUNCHTIME.

MULTIGRAIN QUINOA MUESLI

The good thing about making your own muesli is that you can tweak the combinations to taste.
This version is gluten-free, but you can swap cornflakes for wheat or barley flakes if you prefer.

Serves 4

50g/2oz/¹⁄₃ cup hazelnuts
50g/2oz/¹⁄₄ cup pumpkin seeds
50g/2oz/¹⁄₂ cup quinoa flakes
25g/1oz/1 cup quinoa pops
50g/2oz/1 cup crisped rice
  cereal
25g/1oz/²⁄₃ cup cornflakes
25g/1oz/¹⁄₆ cup dried
  blueberries
25g/1oz/¹⁄₆ cup dried
  cranberries
natural (plain) yogurt and
  honey, or milk and fresh fruit,
  to serve

COOK'S TIP
Quinoa pops are available
in health stores and online.

Gluten Free; Energy 333kcal/1398kJ;
Protein 8g; Carbohydrate 43g, of which
sugars 11g; Fat 15g, of which saturates 2g;
Cholesterol 0mg; Calcium 94mg; Fibre 0g;
Sodium 150mg.

Under a medium grill (broiler), toast the hazelnuts and pumpkin seeds
for a few minutes until the seeds start to pop and the nuts are browning.
Watch the nuts closely, as it is easy to scorch them.

Roughly crush the toasted hazelnuts with the end of a rolling pin.
Set aside to cool completely.

Mix the cooled nuts and seeds with the remaining ingredients in a
large bowl and store in an airtight container. Serve in a bowl, with
yogurt and honey, or milk and fresh fruit.

SALMON AND QUINOA FRITTATA

Quinoa can replace the traditional potato in this Italian dish and, with a useful amount of watercress and salmon, this makes a hearty one-dish brunch. Any leftovers can be eaten cold in a packed lunch.

Serves 4

15ml/1 tbsp olive oil
1 medium onion, finely diced
1 orange or red (bell) pepper, chopped
2 cloves garlic, crushed
5ml/1 tsp fennel seeds (optional)
75g/3oz watercress or rocket (arugula), roughly chopped
30ml/2 tbsp crème fraîche
6 eggs, beaten
a handful of parsley, finely chopped
100g/3¾oz smoked salmon, cut into thin strips
115g/4oz/⅔ cup cooked red quinoa
50g/2oz/½ cup grated Parmesan
salt and ground black pepper

Gluten Free; Energy 310kcal/1289kJ; Protein 22g; Carbohydrate 13g, of which sugars 6g; Fat 19g, of which saturates 7g; Cholesterol 237mg; Calcium 228mg; Fibre 2g; Sodium 664mg.

Heat the oil in a heavy frying pan or skillet and add the onion and chopped pepper. Stir-fry for 8–10 minutes until the onion is soft, then add the garlic and fennel seeds, and cook for 2 minutes.

Add the watercress or rocket and cook for a few more minutes until the leaves have wilted.

Meanwhile, whisk together the crème fraîche, beaten egg, herbs and seasoning in a small bowl.

Add the salmon and quinoa to the frying pan, mix well, then spread evenly over the base of the pan.

Pour the beaten egg mixture into the pan, lower the heat, and cook for 5–8 minutes until the frittata is cooked most of the way through (you can test this by carefully pressing the top with a fork). Covering the pan with a lid will help ensure even cooking. Heat the grill (broiler) to medium.

Sprinkle the grated cheese over the top of the frittata, then place under the grill, making sure the handle is not exposed to heat, for 3–5 minutes until the frittata is puffed and golden brown. Serve warm or at room temperature.

OAT AND CINNAMON BREAKFAST ROLLS

The combination of sugar and cinnamon is perfect at breakfast. You can prepare these rolls the night before, keeping the shaped, uncooked dough in the refrigerator overnight for baking in the morning.

Makes 12

350g/12oz/3 cups strong white
    bread flour
115g/4oz/1 cup quinoa flakes
50g/2oz/scant ½ cup rolled
    oats
7.5ml/1½ tsp salt
30ml/2 tbsp soft light brown
    sugar
10ml/2 tsp ground cinnamon
10ml/2 tsp easy blend (rapid-
    rise) dried yeast
175ml/6fl oz/¾ cup boiled
    water
175ml/6fl oz/¾ cup milk
a little milk and 10ml/2 tsp soft
    light brown sugar, to glaze
butter and clear honey or fresh
    fruit, to serve

COOK'S TIP
You can use a breadmaker on a basic wholegrain programme to make these.

Sift the flour into a large bowl, then stir in the quinoa flakes, oats, salt, sugar, cinnamon and dried yeast. Make a well in the centre.

Mix the boiled water with the milk to make a lukewarm liquid, then add this to the dry ingredients, stirring to form a pliable dough. Transfer the dough to a floured board and knead for 5–8 minutes by holding the dough with one hand and stretching it with the palm of the other hand. Turn the dough and repeat this action until the dough is smooth and elastic. Alternatively, knead with a dough hook in an electric mixer for 3–4 minutes.

Place the dough in a lightly oiled bowl, cover with a damp cloth and leave in a warm place for 1–1½ hours, until nearly doubled in size.

Knock back (punch down) the dough and knead for a further few minutes by hand, or with an electric dough hook.

Divide the dough into 12 rolls, plaiting (braiding) or shaping them as desired. Place on greased baking sheets.

Glaze the rolls with milk, sprinkle with light brown sugar and leave to prove for a further 20 minutes in a warm place. Preheat the oven to 220°C/425°F/Gas 7. Or, if you want to cook them fresh for breakfast the next morning, place the trays in the refrigerator at this point.

Bake for 12–15 minutes, until the rolls are risen and golden and sound hollow when tapped. Allow to cool on a wire rack for 15 minutes. They are delicious served warm with clear honey and a platter of fresh fruit. If cooking the next morning, remove from the refrigerator and bring to room temperature while the oven heats.

Per 2 rolls: Energy 330kcal/1397kJ; Protein 12g; Carbohydrate 65g, of which sugars 8g; Fat 4g, of which saturates 1g; Cholesterol 4mg; Calcium 162mg; Fibre 2g; Sodium 462mg.

LEMON AND RAISIN PANCAKES

Making pancakes is a great way to start the weekend. Those tucking in won't notice any difference between these and regular pancakes, happily oblivious to the nutritional boost they are getting.

Makes 16

1 egg
120ml/4fl oz/½ cup natural (plain) yogurt
120ml/4fl oz/½ cup milk
115g/4oz/1 cup quinoa flour
15ml/1 tbsp baking powder
50g/2oz/¼ cup sugar
grated rind of 1 lemon
25g/1oz/⅕ cup raisins
vegetable oil, for frying
butter and maple syrup, to serve

Whisk the egg, yogurt and milk until combined. Put the flour and baking powder into a large bowl and make a well in the middle.

Add the egg mixture to the well and use a whisk to incorporate the flour mixture, a little at a time, to make a smooth batter. Add the sugar and lemon rind. Allow to stand for 20 minutes.

When you are ready to cook, pour a little oil into a frying pan or pancake pan and use kitchen paper to spread it evenly over the base.

Place the pan over medium heat, and when hot spoon in enough batter to form two or three pancakes, about 6–7.5cm/2½–3in in diameter.

Sprinkle a few raisins on each pancake and cook for 1–2 minutes on each side.

When the pancakes are puffed and bubbly, and golden on both sides, remove from the pan, top with a knob of butter, and keep warm while you cook the remaining batter. Serve the pancakes warm with extra butter, if you wish, and maple syrup poured over.

Gluten free; Energy 258kcal/1088kJ; Protein 6g; Carbohydrate 42g, of which sugars 20g; Fat 9g, of which saturates 3g; Cholesterol 34mg; Calcium 99mg; Fibre 2g; Sodium 45mg.

VARIATIONS
• Replace the raisins with fresh blueberries, if you wish.
• Try serving the pancakes with some crispy grilled (broiled) bacon for a traditional American breakfast.

BREAKFAST BARS WITH QUINOA POWERSHAKE

Perfect for when you are short of time, take a portable powershake and breakfast bar with you. Together, these give you a healthy, low-glycaemic, high-calcium and protein-rich start to the day.

Makes 8

For the breakfast bars

150ml/¼ pint/⅔ cup clear honey

40g/1½oz/3 tbsp butter

45ml/3 tbsp demerara (raw) sugar

2 small or 1 large eating apple, peeled and grated

30ml/2 tbsp puffed quinoa

30ml/2 tbsp ground flaxseeds (linseeds)

30ml/2 tbsp chopped hazelnuts

2.5ml/½ tsp ground cloves

5ml/1 tsp mixed (apple pie) spice

10ml/2 tsp ground ginger

For the quinoa powershake

1 banana, peeled and sliced

200ml/7fl oz/scant 1 cup milk

115g/4oz/½ cup Greek (US strained plain) yogurt

30ml/2 tbsp quinoa flakes

5ml/1 tsp honey

a pinch each of ground nutmeg and cinnamon

Heat the oven to 180°C/350°F/Gas 4. Grease a 18cm/7in square baking tin (pan), and line with baking parchment.

In a large pan over low heat, heat the honey, butter and sugar, stirring, until the sugar has dissolved, and you have a thin syrup.

Remove the pan from the heat and stir in the remaining ingredients, until thoroughly combined. Transfer to the prepared tin and spread evenly into the edges with the back of a fork.

Bake for 30–35 minutes until crisp at the edges. Score into eight bars with a sharp knife while still warm, but leave in the tin until totally cool. Store in an airtight container.

For the Quinoa Powershake: Blend all of the ingredients in a blender or food processor until smooth.

Pour into a glass and drink immediately, or transfer into a portable vessel and take it with you for a breakfast on the move.

Breakfast Bars: Gluten Free; Energy 174kcal/731kJ; Protein 2g; Carbohydrate 26g, of which sugars 22g; Fat 8g, of which saturates 2g; Cholesterol 10mg; Calcium 16mg; Fibre 1g; Sodium 35mg.
Powershake: Gluten free; Energy 491kcal/2050kJ; Protein 18g; Carbohydrate 56g, of which sugars 37g; Fat 21g, of which saturates 13g; Cholesterol 47mg; Calcium 419mg; Fibre 5g; Sodium 170mg.

FRESH TOMATO AND BLACK QUINOA SOUP

This lovely spicy soup is brimming with nutrients: heart-healthy antioxidants like lycopene and beta carotene, and vitamin C, together with low-GI lentils and quinoa.

Serves 4

30ml/2 tbsp vegetable oil
1 medium onion, roughly
    chopped
3 cloves garlic, crushed
10ml/2 tsp harissa (chilli sauce)
12 plum tomatoes (about
    675g/1½lb), roughly
    chopped
175g/6oz/1 cup black quinoa
175g/6oz/¾ cup red lentils
30ml/2 tbsp sun-dried
    tomatoes, roughly chopped
1.75 litres/3 pints/7½ cups
    vegetable stock
salt and ground black pepper

To serve

5ml/1 tsp harissa
30ml/2 tbsp natural (plain)
    yogurt
1 sun-dried tomato, finely
    chopped
warmed crusty bread

Heat the oil in a large pan, then add the chopped onion and garlic. Cook for 2–3 minutes on a medium heat, stirring, until softened.

Stir the harissa into the onions, then add the chopped tomatoes and cook for a further 5 minutes on a lower heat to release the aromatic flavours from the harissa into the vegetables.

Add the quinoa, lentils, sun-dried tomatoes and stock, then bring to the boil. Lower the heat, cover, and simmer for 12–14 minutes, until the quinoa is soft to bite and the lentils are tender. Season to taste with salt and pepper and add a little more harissa if you wish.

In a small bowl, swirl together, but don't completely mix, the yogurt and harissa for serving.

Pour the soup into four warmed bowls and top with a spoonful of the harissa yogurt. Sprinkle a few chopped sun-dried tomatoes on top and serve with warmed crusty bread.

Gluten free with GF free stock; Energy 257kcal/1084kJ; Protein 11g; Carbohydrate 41g, of which sugars 12g; Fat 7g, of which saturates 1g; Cholesterol 0mg; Calcium 150mg; Fibre 6g; Sodium 583mg.

EDAMAME BEAN DIP WITH PARMESAN STRAWS

This delightful, creamy dip, served with crispy Parmesan pastry straws, would make a perfect beginning to a drinks party or summer barbecue.

Serves 4

For the Parmesan straws

75g/3oz/⅔ cup wholemeal
    (whole-wheat) flour
75g/3oz/¾ cup quinoa flakes
75g/3oz/1 cup grated Parmesan
    cheese, plus extra for
    sprinkling
75g/3oz/6 tbsp butter, softened
cold water, to bind
milk, for glazing
paprika, for sprinkling

**For the edamame bean and
chive dip**

75g/3oz/½ cup frozen
    edamame beans, cooked
50g/2oz/⅓ cup pearl quinoa,
    cooked
60ml/4 tbsp sour cream
60ml/4 tbsp mayonnaise
30ml/2 tbsp fresh chives,
    chopped, plus extra for
    garnishing
15ml/1 tbsp fresh coriander
    (cilantro), roughly chopped
salt and ground black pepper
paprika, for sprinkling

For the Parmesan straws, place the flour and quinoa flakes in a large bowl and mix with the grated Parmesan.

Add the butter and, using your fingertips, rub in the fat until the mixture resembles fine breadcrumbs. Add just enough water to bind everything into a firm dough.

Wrap the dough in clear film (plastic wrap) and chill in the refrigerator for 30 minutes. Heat the oven to 180°C/ 350°F/Gas 4.

Line a baking tray with baking parchment. On a floured board, roll the pastry into a rectangle shape and score into 'straw' shapes, about 2 x 5cm/¾ x 2in.

Brush the pastry straws with milk, then sprinkle with grated Parmesan and a little paprika. Press the cheese gently with your fingertips to help it adhere to the pastry, then carefully transfer the straws to the lined baking tray. Bake for 10–12 minutes, until golden and crisp. Transfer to a wire rack to cool.

Meanwhile, prepare the dip by blending all the ingredients in a food processor until smooth and creamy.

Transfer to a bowl, sprinkle with chives and a little paprika, and serve with the warm Parmesan straws.

Straws per 4 straws: Energy 344kcal/1433kJ; Protein 12g; Carbohydrate 24g, of which sugars 1g; Fat 23g, of which saturates 14g; Cholesterol 57mg; Calcium 225mg; Fibre 2g; Sodium 260mg.
Edamame bean and chive dip: Gluten free with GF mayonnaise. Energy 169kcal/700kJ; Protein 4g; Carbohydrate 4g, of which sugars 1g; Fat 15g, of which saturates; 40g; Cholesterol 20mg; Calcium 37mg; Fibre 1g; Sodium 72mg.

SHIITAKE MUSHROOM AND SESAME SALAD

A mixture of shiitake and dried porcini mushrooms and tricolour quinoa results in a vibrant salad, an opulent sesame taste and a very useful profile of vitamins, antioxidants, iron and calcium.

Serves 4

12g/½oz dried porcini
  mushrooms
175g/6oz/1 cup tricolour
  quinoa
475ml/16fl oz/2 cups water
15ml/1 tbsp sesame oil
1 clove garlic, crushed
2cm/1in piece fresh root ginger,
  peeled and finely chopped
1 red and 1 orange (bell)
  pepper, sliced in thin strips
115g/4oz shiitake mushrooms,
  roughly torn
30ml/2 tbsp sesame seeds
salt and ground black pepper

For the dressing

5ml/1 tsp toasted sesame oil
15ml/1 tbsp rice vinegar
2.5ml/½ tsp Dijon mustard

To serve

1 small Little Gem (Bibb)
  lettuce, leaves separated
¼ cucumber, sliced into thin
  strips

Bring the porcini mushrooms, quinoa and water to the boil in a medium pan, lower the heat and simmer for 12–14 minutes. Drain, discarding any excess water, and set aside to cool.

In another pan, heat the sesame oil, add the garlic, ginger and peppers and stir-fry until the peppers are softened.

Add the shiitake mushrooms and cook for a further 3–4 minutes, until the mushrooms are lightly browned.

Dry roast the sesame seeds in a frying pan for 2–3 minutes, until they are just browned and fragrant, regularly turning to prevent them from burning.

In a large bowl, mix together the cooked quinoa and porcini mushrooms, the pepper and mushroom mixture and the toasted seeds. Leave to cool.

Make the dressing by shaking the ingredients together in a sealed container, or whisking in a small bowl.

Pour the dressing over the cooled salad. Serve in bowls lined with lettuce leaves accompanied by wedges of crisp, salted cucumber.

Gluten free; Energy 287kcal/1203kJ; Protein 10g; Carbohydrate 36g, of which sugars 8g; Fat 13g, of which saturates 2g; Cholesterol 0mg; Calcium 113mg; Fibre 6g; Sodium 51mg.

TOASTED GRAIN, FENNEL AND ORANGE SALAD

Wholegrains such as quinoa and buckwheat are absorbed more slowly than refined grains, so they keep you satisfied for longer. They are easy to prepare, and toasting them gives a richer flavour.

Serves 4

75g/3oz/⅓ cup wheatberries
175ml/6fl oz/¾ cup boiling water
75g/3oz/½ cup pearled spelt
75g/3oz/½ cup buckwheat
115g/4oz/⅔ cup red quinoa, rinsed
750ml/1¼ pints/3 cups vegetable stock
50g/2oz/½ cup blanched whole almonds, cut in half
1 fennel bulb, outer leaves removed, finely sliced
1 orange, peeled and segmented, all white pith removed
a good handful of parsley, finely chopped
rocket (arugula) or lettuce leaves, to serve

For the dressing

60ml/4 tbsp olive oil
30ml/2 tbsp cider vinegar
5ml/1 tsp wholegrain mustard
ground black pepper

Place the wheatberries in a small pan and dry-fry for 4–6 minutes, until lightly browned. Add the boiling water, being careful as it hits the hot pan, and simmer for 35–40 minutes until the wheatberries are tender to bite. Drain, discarding any excess water.

Meanwhile, in large pan, dry-fry the spelt, buckwheat and quinoa for 4–6 minutes, stirring, until lightly browned. Add the vegetable stock to the pan and simmer for 20–25 minutes, until the grains are tender to bite.

Meanwhile, toast the almonds under a medium grill (broiler) for 6–8 minutes, until lightly browned. Watch them all the time as it is easy to scorch them.

Make the dressing by shaking the ingredients together in a jar, or whisking together in a small bowl.

Mix the cooked wheatberries with the other warm grains in a large bowl. Add the toasted almonds along with the fennel, orange and parsley. Pour over the dressing and toss through gently.

Serve immediately on a bed of fresh rocket or lettuce leaves.

> **COOK'S TIP**
> Wheatberries take nearly twice as long to cook compared to the other grains so need to be prepared separately.

Energy 520kcal/2177kJ; 16g; Carbohydrate 61g, of which sugars 4g; Fat 25g, of which saturates 3g; Cholesterol 7mg; Calcium 75mg; Fibre 5g; Sodium 361mg.

FISH AND MEAT MAINS

ADDING QUINOA TO MEAT OR FISH HELPS TO
MAKE IT GO FURTHER, BOTH IN TERMS OF BULK
AND NUTRITION. THE RECIPES HERE ARE PACKED
WITH PROTEIN, ESSENTIAL AMINO ACIDS,
VITAMINS AND MINERALS, AND OFFER MANY
WAYS TO ADD QUINOA TO YOUR FOOD.

CHINESE PRAWNS WITH EGG-FRIED QUINOA

This is a dish in which Asia meets South America with mouthwatering effect. The stir-fry is a delicious mix of hot, sweet and salty flavours that brings the mild-tasting quinoa, egg and prawns to life.

Serves 4

450g/1lb cooked, peeled king prawns (jumbo shrimp)
30ml/2 tbsp sesame oil
60ml/4 tbsp vegetable oil
1 medium chilli, finely chopped
2 cloves garlic, crushed
6 spring onions (scallions), finely sliced
250g/9oz/2 cups mushrooms, finely sliced
125g/5oz/1¼ cups frozen peas
600g/1lb 6oz/4 cups cooked white quinoa
6 eggs, beaten

For the marinade

120ml/4fl oz/½ cup soy sauce
30ml/2 tbsp sesame seed oil
60ml/4 tbsp sweet chilli oil

Gluten free with GF soy sauce; Energy 691kcal/2741kJ; Protein 39g; Carbohydrate 40g, of which sugars 8g; Fat 40g, of which saturates 7g; Cholesterol 192mg; Calcium 169mg; Fibre 8g; Sodium 2766mg.

Mix the prawns into the marinade, cover and set aside for 2 hours.

Heat the oils in a frying pan or wok. Add the chilli and garlic and stir-fry for 5 seconds. Add the spring onions, mushrooms and peas, and continue to stir-fry until golden. Add the quinoa and toss through.

Meanwhile, place the prawns and marinade in a medium pan on high heat and cook the prawns for 5 minutes.

Make a well in the centre of the stir-fried mixture and pour in the beaten eggs, allowing the heat to start cooking them from underneath for a couple of minutes. Lower the heat slightly and quickly mix the semi-cooked egg with the other ingredients to finish cooking for a few seconds. Do not overcook or the egg will become rubbery.

Add the prawns and marinade, remove from the heat and serve.

QUINOA-STUFFED TROUT

The lovely tangy flavour of sumac offsets the rich oiliness of trout, which is stuffed with quinoa, dried fruit and herbs. Serve any leftover stuffing with the fish.

Serves 4

30ml/2 tbsp olive oil
1 medium onion, finely diced
1 clove garlic, crushed
30ml/2 tbsp sumac
2.5ml/½ tsp ground cinnamon
550ml/18fl oz/2½ cups fish stock
juice and rind of 1 lemon
175g/6oz/1 cup pearl quinoa
50g/2oz/⅓ cup finely chopped dried apricots
50g/2oz/⅓ cup raisins
4 small whole trout (about 1kg/2¼lb total weight), cleaned and descaled
salt and ground black pepper
finely cut lemon rind shreds and fresh watercress leaves, to garnish
roasted potatoes and green salad, to serve

Gluten free with GF fish stock; Energy 478kcal/2008kJ; Protein 37g; Carbohydrate 45g, of which sugars 18g; Fat 18g, of which saturates 3g; Cholesterol 98mg; Calcium 97mg; Fibre 7g; Sodium 494mg.

Heat the oven to 180°C/350°F/Gas 4. Heat 15ml/1 tbsp of the olive oil in a medium pan and add the onion, garlic, sumac and cinnamon.

Fry for a few minutes to soften the onion and release the spice flavours. Add the stock to the pan with the lemon juice and rind, and stir in the quinoa.

Bring to the boil and simmer for 8 minutes. Add the apricots and raisins, and simmer for a further few minutes until the quinoa is cooked and the fruit plump. Season to taste.

Pat the fish dry with kitchen paper. Brush the skin with the remaining oil and lay the whole fish on a board to enable stuffing. Fill each fish with the fruited quinoa mix. Place the fish in a serving dish and cover with foil.

Bake for 20–30 minutes, until the fish is light pink and flaky. Dry-fry leftover stuffing in a frying pan to reheat.

Garnish the fish with lemon rind shreds and serve with the reheated stuffing, roasted potatoes and salad.

MOROCCAN CHICKEN CASSEROLE

This tagine-style casserole of spiced meat and vegetables is packed with North African flavours. It is marvellous as a filling one-pot meal for many hungry mouths.

Serves 4

30ml/2 tbsp vegetable oil
450g/1lb chicken thighs
6 shallots, peeled and cut in half
2 garlic cloves, crushed
2.5cm/1in piece of fresh root
    ginger, grated
7.5ml/1½ tsp smoked paprika
7.5ml/1½ tsp ground cumin
225g/8oz butternut squash,
    peeled and cut into cubes
300g/12oz/2 cups pearl quinoa
115g/4oz/scant 1 cup cooked
    chickpeas
200g/7oz canned tomatoes
50g/2oz/½ cup black olives,
    pitted
1 preserved lemon, finely
    chopped
25g/1oz/¼ cup raisins
30ml/2 tbsp tomato purée
    (paste)
1.2 litres/2 pints/5 cups chicken
    stock
salt and ground black pepper
torn fresh coriander (cilantro),
    to garnish
fresh bread, to serve

Heat the oven to 180°C/350°F/Gas 4. Heat 15ml/1 tbsp of the vegetable oil in a large frying pan and add the chicken thighs, sealing them over a high heat for a few minutes until lightly browned all over. Transfer to a large lidded casserole.

Add a further 15ml/1 tbsp oil to the frying pan and add the shallots, garlic, fresh ginger, paprika, cumin and butternut squash. Fry for around 5–6 minutes to release the flavours and soften the vegetables.

Add the quinoa, chickpeas, tomatoes, olives, lemon and raisins and stir to heat through and coat the quinoa. Transfer the mixture to the casserole, then place over medium heat.

Add the tomato purée, stock and seasoning to the casserole and bring to a simmer, then cover and cook in the oven for 50–60 minutes, until the squash is tender and most of the juices have been absorbed by the quinoa. Remove the casserole from the oven and stir in the torn fresh coriander.

Serve in warmed bowls with chunks of fresh bread. Don't leave the casserole to stand for too long, as the quinoa will continue to absorb the cooking liquid.

Energy 678kcal/2846kJ; Protein 36g; Carbohydrate 72g, of which sugars 16g; Fat 30g, of which saturates 6g; Cholesterol 123mg; Calcium 162mg; Fibre 7g; Sodium 739mg.

FIVE-SPICE PORK AND APPLE PATTIES

These delicious patties are great for a quick supper dish or a barbecue, served with pak choi and cooked quinoa with shallots and garlic. Have some cooked quinoa handy for ease of preparation.

Serves 4
vegetable oil, for frying
1 medium onion, finely chopped
2 cloves garlic, crushed
1 medium cooking apple,
*   peeled, cored and grated*
450g/1lb minced (ground) lean
*   pork*
10ml/2 tsp Chinese five-spice
*   powder*
5ml/1 tsp mustard
115g/4oz/²/₃ cup cooked red or
*   black quinoa*
1 egg, beaten
50g/2oz/½ cup quinoa flour
salt and ground black pepper
steamed pak choi (bok choy)
*   and soy sauce, to serve*

For the shallot and garlic
quinoa mix
40g/1½ oz/¼ cup pearl quinoa
vegetable oil for frying
1 banana shallot, finely chopped
1 garlic clove, crushed

Heat 15ml/1 tbsp oil in a medium frying pan. Add the onion, garlic and apple and fry for 3–4 minutes, until softened. Remove from the heat and transfer to a large bowl.

Add the minced pork, five-spice powder and mustard to the bowl, together with the cooked quinoa, beaten egg, flour and seasoning. Use your hands to mix the ingredients together until well combined.

With slightly dampened hands, to help prevent sticking, shape the mince mixture into eight burger-size 'patties' and set them aside on a floured board.

Wash and dry the frying pan, heat 30ml/2 tbsp oil in the pan and fry the patties on high heat for 3–4 minutes.

Flip the patties and fry on the other side for another 3 minutes, then reduce the heat and cook for a further 6–8 minutes, until cooked through and no longer pink in the middle. Keep warm in the oven.

To make the quinoa accompaniment, cook the required amount of quinoa and, while it is steaming, fry a finely chopped banana shallot on high heat until golden and crispy. Add the crushed garlic clove and stir for a few seconds to release the aroma, then stir the onion and garlic mixture into the cooked quinoa, adding salt and pepper to taste.

Serve the patties on the shallot and garlic quinoa mix, with steamed pak choi and a dash of soy sauce.

Gluten free; Energy 766kcal/3167kJ; Protein 16g; Carbohydrate 22g, of which sugars 6g; Fat 69g, of which saturates 24g; Cholesterol   113mg; Calcium 70mg; Fibre 3g; Sodium 105mg.

LAMB AND BLACK QUINOA PILAFF

In this Middle Eastern-inspired pilaff black quinoa replaces the rice, and is cooked in a rich, spicy tomato stock with colourful vegetables to make a striking dish.

Serves 4

2.5ml/½ tsp coriander seeds
5ml/1 tsp cumin seeds
15ml/1 tbsp olive oil
1 medium onion, finely diced
300g/11oz minced (ground) lamb
1 clove garlic, peeled and crushed
1 small aubergine (eggplant), chopped
1 red (bell) pepper, chopped
25g/1oz/¼ cup pitted black olives
275g/10oz/1⅔ cups black quinoa
250ml/8fl oz/1 cup water
450g/1lb canned chopped tomatoes
30ml/2 tbsp tomato purée (paste)
1 lamb or chicken stock (bouillon) cube
3 cardamom pods, bruised
2 bay leaves
salt and ground black pepper
natural (plain) yogurt, and green salad, to serve

In a small pan, dry-fry the coriander and cumin seeds on high heat for 1–2 minutes to release their flavours. Grind using a mortar and pestle or whizz briefly in a coffee grinder.

Add the oil and onion to a large frying pan and fry for 3 minutes on medium heat to soften the onion.

Add the lamb to the pan and fry on high heat for 3–4 minutes before adding the ground seeds, garlic, aubergine, pepper and olives.

Stir-fry for another 3–4 minutes. The lamb juices released will be absorbed by the aubergine, but you could drain them off for a less fatty dish, if you wish.

Add the rinsed quinoa, water, chopped tomatoes, tomato purée, stock cube, cardamom pods and bay leaves to the pan, season well with salt and pepper.

Bring to the boil, reduce the heat and gently simmer for 20 minutes until most of the liquid is absorbed and the quinoa is soft but still with some bite.

Leave the pilaff to stand for about 5–10 minutes before serving. Remove the bay leaves, and the cardamom pods if you can find them.

Serve the pilaff drizzled with natural yogurt to offset the naturally rich lamb, along with crisp salad leaves.

Energy 488kcal/2042kJ; Protein 28g; Carbohydrate 54g, of which sugars 12g; Fat 19g, of which saturates 6g; Cholesterol 57mg; Calcium 152mg; Fibre 8g; Sodium 560mg.

VEGETARIAN MAINS

QUINOA IS PERHAPS ONE OF THE MOST
PERFECT NON-ANIMAL SOURCES OF PROTEIN,
CONTAINING ALL NINE ESSENTIAL AMINO ACIDS.
AS THE RECIPES HERE CLEARLY SHOW, QUINOA
REALLY COMES INTO ITS OWN AS THE MAIN
INGREDIENT IN VEGETARIAN DISHES.

MUSHROOM QUINOA RISOTTO

Quinoa makes a pleasing change to traditional arborio rice. Unlike risotto there is no need for constant stirring between additions of stock, so it doesn't require undivided attention.

Serves 4

30ml/2 tbsp olive oil
300g/12oz/2 cups red quinoa
10 spring onions (scallions),
  finely sliced
3 cloves garlic, peeled and
  crushed
1 litre/1¾ pints/4 cups
  vegetable stock
300g/11oz/4 cups chopped
  chestnut mushrooms
25g/1oz/2 tbsp butter
60ml/4 tbsp double (heavy)
  cream
115g/4oz Parmesan cheese
  shavings
fresh parsley, chopped, to
  garnish
salt and ground black pepper

Gluten free with GF stock; Energy
568kcal/2372kJ; Protein 22g; Carbohydrate
51g, of which sugars 6g; Fat 32g, of which
saturates 14g; Cholesterol 57mg; Calcium
397mg; Fibre 7g; Sodium 535mg.

Heat the oil in a heavy pan and add the quinoa, spring onions and garlic. Fry, stirring, for 3–4 minutes until softened.

Add half of the stock and bring to the boil. Lower the heat and simmer for about 5 minutes, stirring occasionally.

Add the chopped mushrooms to the pan with the remainder of the stock and cook for about 8–10 minutes, until the quinoa is soft but retains a little firmness for texture.

Add further boiling water if required to keep the risotto moist.

Stir in the butter, cream, salt if needed, and black pepper to taste. Serve on warmed plates, sprinkled with shaved Parmesan cheese and chopped parsley.

MALAYSIAN TOFU AND QUINOA LAKSA

Laksa is a Malay/Singaporean curry of which there are many variants. Here the noodles are substituted with pearl quinoa to create a substantial and mouthwatering lunch or supper dish.

Serves 4

10ml/2 tbsp vegetable oil
10ml/2 tbsp red curry paste
150g/5oz sweet potato, peeled and cubed
125g/4¼oz/¾ cup pearl quinoa
300ml/½ pint/1¼ cups coconut milk
600ml/20 fl oz/ 2 cups water
15ml/1 tbsp tamarind paste
1 clove garlic, crushed
25g/1oz spring onions (scallions), cut into 5mm/¼in slices
8 mangetouts (snow peas)
4 baby corn, cut in half
200g/7oz tofu, cut into 2cm/¾in square cubes
fresh coriander (cilantro), chopped, and a 6cm/2½in piece of cucumber cut into thin matchsticks, to garnish
green tea, to serve

Heat 15ml/1 tbsp oil in a large pan, then add the curry paste, sweet potato cubes and quinoa. Fry on medium heat for 3–4 minutes, until the spice fragrances and flavours are released.

Add the coconut milk to the pan and stir until smooth, then add the water and tamarind paste. Bring to the boil, then lower the heat and simmer for 12–14 minutes, stirring occasionally, until the quinoa is tender.

Drain the quinoa, cover to keep warm and set aside, reserving the curried coconut stock in a small pan. Do not leave the quinoa in the stock or it will continue to absorb the fluid and swell.

In a frying pan, heat the remaining oil and add the garlic, spring onions, mangetouts and baby corn. Stir-fry on high heat for 3–4 minutes, until softened but still crisp.

Add the tofu cubes to the frying pan and sear for a further 3 minutes, gently turning the cubes only once or twice to avoid breaking them. Reheat the coconut stock.

To serve, divide the tofu and vegetables and the quinoa mixture between four large warmed bowls, and pour over the hot stock. Garnish with fresh coriander leaves and cucumber matchsticks. Serve with green tea to cool your senses.

Gluten free; Energy 266kcal/1121kJ; Protein 12g; Carbohydrate 38g, of which sugars 12g; Fat 8g, of which saturates 1g; Cholesterol 0mg; Calcium 264mg; Fibre 4g; Sodium 152mg.

BEAN CREOLE QUINOA JAMBALAYA

Jambalaya originated in the Caribbean and usually contains meat and rice, but here quinoa and vegetables are cooked with stock and spices until wonderfully tender.

Serves 4

30ml/2 tbsp vegetable oil
1 onion, roughly chopped
2 cloves garlic, crushed
1 dried chilli, finely chopped
5ml/1 tsp ground paprika
5ml/1 tsp ground cayenne
    pepper
1 red (bell) pepper, deseeded
    and cut into thin strips
1 small aubergine (eggplant),
    cut into 1cm/½in wide slices
2 celery stick, chopped into
    1cm/½in pieces
2 tomatoes, cut into wedges
115g/4oz/scant 1 cup drained
    canned butter (lima) beans
275g/10oz/1⅔ cups pearl
    quinoa
1 litre/1¾ pints/4 cups
    vegetable stock
15ml/1 tbsp tomato purée
    (paste)
salt and ground black pepper
60ml/4 tbsp sour cream and
    30ml/2 tbsp grated cheese, to
    serve

Put the oil, onion, garlic, chilli and spices in a wide pan or casserole dish and fry for 4–5 minutes on medium heat to release the spicy flavours. Be careful not to over-brown the onion.

Add the pepper, aubergine and celery and heat with the spice mixture for a further 5 minutes, turning occasionally, until the vegetables start to soften. Add the tomatoes, butter beans, quinoa, stock, tomato purée and seasoning and bring to the boil.

Lower the heat and simmer for around 14–16 minutes, until the quinoa is tender to bite but there is still a little stock remaining.

To serve, ladle the jambalaya into deep bowls. Drizzle each with a spoonful of sour cream and a sprinkling of grated cheese.

Energy 464kcal/1939kJ; Protein 16g; Carbohydrate 62g, of which sugars 12g; Fat 18g, of which saturates 5g; Cholesterol 16mg; Calcium 167mg; Fibre 7g; Sodium 434mg.

ROCKET QUINOA PASTA WITH PANGRATTATO

Pangrattato is flavoured, crisp breadcrumbs, used in Italy to add texture and taste. You can make a larger batch of this fiery quinoa version for adding a kick to salads or pasta dishes.

Serves 4
400g/14oz quinoa pasta
15ml/1 tbsp olive oil
2 cloves garlic, crushed
75g/3oz rocket (arugula),
 roughly chopped
300ml/½ pint/1¼ cups crème
 fraîche
125g/4¼oz mozzarella balls
salt and ground black pepper

For the hot fennel
pangrattato
30ml/2 tbsp chilli oil
5ml/1 tsp fennel seeds
2 cloves garlic, crushed
½ small dried chilli, crumbled
30ml/2 tbsp pine nuts
150g/5oz/scant 1 cup cooked
 white quinoa
salt and ground black pepper

Gluten free; Energy 931kcal/3893kJ;
Protein 22g; Carbohydrate 94g, of which
sugars 3g; Fat 55g, of which saturates 27g;
Cholesterol 102mg; Calcium 244mg; Fibre
3g; Sodium 141mg.

First prepare the pangrattato. Heat the chilli oil in a small pan and add the spices, pine nuts and quinoa. Cook, stirring constantly, for 5–8 minutes until crisp and brown. Season to taste, then set aside.

Cook the pasta for about 15 minutes, in a large pan of boiling water, stirring occasionally to prevent sticking.

Meanwhile make the pasta sauce. Heat the olive oil in a medium pan and add the garlic and rocket, cooking for 1–2 minutes until the rocket has wilted. Add the crème fraîche and heat until warmed through. Season with plenty of salt and pepper.

Drain the cooked pasta and return to the pan, add the mozzarella balls and then stir in the hot sauce. Divide the pasta between warmed bowls. Sprinkle each serving with a teaspoon of pangrattato, serving the remainder in a bowl at the table for people to help themselves.

VEGETABLES WITH A QUINOA AND CHEESE CRUST

This dish uses carbohydrate-rich root vegetables bathed in cream and Parmesan cheese, and contains a mouthwatering range of soft and crunchy textures and sweet and savoury flavours.

Serves 4

1 small onion, finely diced
1 clove garlic, crushed
15ml/1 tbsp vegetable oil
225g/8oz celeriac, peeled and diced into 1cm/½in cubes
225g/8oz sweet potato, peeled and diced into 1cm/½in cubes
225g/8oz parsnip, peeled and diced into 1cm/½in cubes
175ml/6fl oz/¾ cup milk
5ml/1 tsp ground nutmeg
175ml/6fl oz/¾ cup double (heavy) cream
225g/8oz fresh beetroot (beet), peeled and very thinly sliced
salt and ground black pepper
rocket (arugula) salad with a mustard dressing, to serve

For the quinoa and cheese crust

175g/6oz/1 cup cooked quinoa
75ml/5 tbsp grated Parmesan cheese
5ml/1 tsp mixed dried herbs
ground black pepper

Heat the oven to 190°C/375°F/Gas 5. In a large pan, soften the onion and garlic in the vegetable oil over medium heat for 3–4 minutes. Add the celeriac, sweet potato and parsnip and fry on medium heat for a further 3–4 minutes.

Add the milk to the pan, together with the nutmeg and seasoning, stir and then bring the milk to the boil. Cover, lower the heat and simmer for 7–8 minutes, until the vegetables are beginning to soften.

Stir the cream into the vegetables, then transfer to a shallow ovenproof dish and spread out evenly. Arrange the beetroot slices in a layer on top.

Make the quinoa and cheese crust by mixing together the ingredients in a bowl, with a good grinding of black pepper. Spread this evenly over the top of the beetroot layer.

Cover the dish with foil and bake in the oven for 20–25 minutes, until the vegetables are soft. Remove the foil and bake for a further 15 minutes to allow the crust to become crisp and golden.

Serve with a peppery rocket salad and a mustard dressing to contrast with the rich, creamy bake.

Gluten free; Energy 550kcal/2289kJ; Protein 16g; Carbohydrate 40g, of which sugars 17g; Fat 38g, of which saturates 21g; Cholesterol 85mg; Calcium 408mg; Fibre 9g; Sodium 352mg.

COOK'S TIP
Keeping the beetroot (beet) slices in a separate layer helps to retain the creamy colour of the sauce. Make sure that the slices are as thin as possible so that they cook completely in the oven.

SPICY BLACK BEAN BURGERS

These burgers use fibre-rich canned black beans. Combined with hot jalapeño peppers, chilli and lime, quinoa adds useful carbohydrate and contributes to a wholesome, rustic texture.

Serves 6

115g/4oz/²⁄₃ cup pearl quinoa
350ml/12fl oz/1½ cups water
30ml/2 tbsp vegetable oil
1 medium onion, finely chopped
1 stick celery, finely chopped
2 cloves garlic, crushed
6 jalapeño peppers, finely chopped
1 red or green chilli, finely chopped
2 medium carrots, peeled and grated
75g/3oz/½ cup roasted peanuts
1 lime, rind and juice
15ml/1 tbsp roughly chopped fresh coriander (cilantro)
400g/14oz can black beans, drained and rinsed
15ml/1 tbsp quinoa flour, for shaping
salt and ground black pepper
burger buns, shredded lettuce, sliced tomato and crème fraîche, to serve

Place the quinoa and water in a medium pan, bring to the boil and simmer for 15–17 minutes until soft.

In another pan heat 15ml/1 tbsp of the oil and add the onion, celery, garlic, jalapeños, chilli and salt and pepper.

Cook for 2–3 minutes on medium heat, then add the grated carrot and cook for 3 minutes. Leave to cool.

Blitz the cooked quinoa, peanuts, lime juice and rind, and fresh coriander in a food processor. Add the beans to the pan and pulse a couple of times to incorporate.

Add the vegetable mixture to the processor and pulse briefly to combine. Test for seasoning. Shape into six burgers, handling lightly, and using quinoa flour as required to stop the mixture from sticking.

Fry the burgers in the remaining 15ml/1 tbsp oil, adding a little more if needed, and turning them halfway through cooking.

Serve in halved rolls with shredded lettuce, sliced tomato and crème fraîche.

Gluten free Energy 296kcal/1243kJ; Protein 13g; Carbohydrate 33g, of which sugars 5g; Fat 14g, of which saturates 2g; Cholesterol 0mg; Calcium 55mg; Fibre 8g; Sodium 68mg.

DESSERTS AND BAKES

MAINLY SEEN AS AN INGREDIENT FOR SAVOURY

DISHES, QUINOA IS ALSO IDEAL FOR BAKING.

IN THIS FINAL CHAPTER YOU WILL FIND RECIPES

USING QUINOA FLOUR, PEARL QUINOA AND

QUINOA FLAKES FOR HEALTHIER PUDDINGS,

DESSERTS AND TEA-TIME TREATS.

PEAR AND HAZELNUT CRUMBLE

A classic fruit crumble is a simple, satisfying and easy dessert to make, and this quinoa version makes a lovely, warming winter pudding. Serve hot or cold, with whipped cream, for an indulgent dessert.

Serves 4

450g/1lb pears
75ml/5 tbsp apple juice
2 star anise
10ml/2 tsp mixed (apple pie) spice
15ml/1 tbsp caster (superfine) sugar
whipped cream or ice cream, to serve

For the crumble topping

75g/3oz/²⁄₃ cup quinoa flour
75g/3oz/²⁄₃ cup quinoa flakes
75g/3oz/6 tbsp soft butter, diced
75g/3oz/6 tbsp soft light brown sugar
50g/2oz hazelnuts, roughly chopped

Preheat the oven to 190°C/375°F/Gas 5. Peel and core the pears, and cut into 2cm/³⁄₄in slices.

Place the pears in an ovenproof dish and add the apple juice, star anise, mixed spice and sugar, stirring to evenly coat the pears.

To make the crumble topping, place the quinoa flour and flakes into a large bowl and, using the tips of your fingers, rub in the soft butter until the mixture resembles coarse breadcrumbs. Use a fork to stir in the sugar and then the chopped hazelnuts.

Sprinkle the crumble mixture evenly over the spiced pears and bake for 25–30 minutes, until the crumble is browned and the pears feel soft when pierced with a sharp knife.

Serve the crumble hot with freshly whipped cream or ice cream.

Gluten free; Energy 486kcal/2034kJ;
Protein 7g; Carbohydrate 61g, of which
sugars 37g; Fat 25g, of which saturates
11g; Cholesterol 9mg; Calcium 92mg; Fibre
3g; Sodium 123mg.

QUINOA PUDDING WITH CHERRY COMPOTE

Quinoa again shows true versatility here in a lovely, creamy milk-based rice dish. In this version, pearl quinoa proves an effective substitute for pudding rice, spiced with aromatic cardamom.

Serves 4

butter, for greasing
6 green cardamom pods
750ml/1¼ pints/3 cups milk
2.5ml/½ tsp ground cinnamon
115g/4oz/²⁄₃ cup pearl quinoa
5ml/1 tsp vanilla extract
50g/2oz/¼ cup demerara (raw) sugar
60ml/4 tbsp double (heavy) cream, plus extra, to serve

For the cherry compote

350g/12oz/1½ cups pitted fresh or frozen cherries
1 orange, strip of rind removed and then squeezed to provide about 150ml/¼ pint/²⁄₃ cup orange juice
50g/2oz/¼ cup caster (superfine) sugar

Gluten free; Energy 460kcal/1933kJ; Protein 11g; Carbohydrate 69g, of which sugars 51g; Fat 17g, of which saturates 10g; Cholesterol 46mg; Calcium 279mg; Fibre 4g; Sodium 95mg.

Heat the oven to 190°C/375°F/Gas 5. Lightly butter a medium ovenproof dish.

With the bottom of a rolling pin, crush the cardamom pods and extract the seeds with the tip of a sharp knife. Discard the husks, then grind the seeds in a mortar and pestle, or in a sturdy bowl with the bottom of the rolling pin.

Pour the milk into a large pan and add the ground cardamom seeds, cinnamon and quinoa. Bring to the boil, then reduce the heat to very low and gently simmer for 10 minutes to infuse the flavours and soften the quinoa.

Remove the pan from the heat and stir in the vanilla extract, sugar and cream, then pour into the prepared dish. Add a little more milk to the mixture if necessary; it should still be loose before it is baked or it will become too dry and solid in the oven.

Bake in the oven for 15–20 minutes, until the top is golden brown and slightly crisp, but the inside is still soft and slightly wobbly.

Meanwhile, prepare the cherry compote. Place the cherries in a pan with the orange rind and juice, and the sugar. Bring to the boil and simmer for 15–20 minutes, until the mixture has a thick syrupy consistency.

To serve, divide the pudding between four dishes. Top with a small spoonful of warm cherry compote and a drizzle of cream.

FROSTED CARROT CAKE

Classic carrot cake should be moist and decadent and this recipe won't disappoint, helped by the addition of olive oil and a good proportion of grated carrot.

Serves 10

175g/6oz/1¾ cup soft light
  brown sugar
115g/4oz/½ cup butter, softened,
  plus extra for greasing
50ml/2fl oz/¼ cup olive oil
3 eggs
115g/4oz/1 cup quinoa flour
75g/3oz/¾ cup ground almonds
5ml/1 tsp baking powder
2.5ml/½ tsp bicarbonate of soda
  (baking soda)
5ml/1 tsp ground cinnamon
2.5ml/½ tsp ground nutmeg
5ml/1 tsp vanilla extract
275g/10oz/2 cups grated carrots
50g/2oz/⅓ cup raisins
30ml/2 tbsp unsweetened cocoa
  powder and 4–5 squares dark
  (bittersweet) chocolate, to
  decorate

For the frosting

350g/12oz/3 cups icing
  (confectioners') sugar
150g/5oz/⅔ cup cream cheese
50g/2oz/¼ cup butter, softened

Preheat the oven to 180°C/350°F/Gas 4. Butter and line a 20cm/8in cake tin (pan).

In a large bowl, using an electric mixer or a hand whisk, beat together the sugar, butter and olive oil until light in colour and fluffy. Add the remaining ingredients and stir to form a batter.

Pour the mixture into the tin and bake for 40–50 minutes, until a skewer comes out clean. Remove from the oven and leave to stand for 10 minutes, then remove the cake from the tin and set aside to cool completely on a wire rack.

Make the frosting by beating together the ingredients until smooth. Decorate the cooled cake with the frosting, creating a swirled effect with the back of a fork. Sift over the cocoa powder and grate the chocolate on top.

Serve in slices, with a cup of tea or coffee. The cake will keep in the refrigerator for up to a week.

Gluten free; Energy 335kcal/1397kJ; Protein 5g; Carbohydrate 33g, of which sugars 24g; Fat 21g, of which saturates 8g; Cholesterol 64mg; Calcium 59mg; Fibre 1g; Sodium 207mg.

ORANGE QUINOA COOKIES

This is a simple, quinoa-rich cookie recipe that will give you lasting satisfaction for those mid-morning or afternoon breaks. They are also great as a nutrition-packed lunch box treat.

Makes 18–20

250g/9oz/1⅛ cups soft butter
175g/6oz/generous 1¾ cup soft light brown sugar
115g/4oz/1 cup quinoa flakes
115g/4oz/1 cup quinoa flour
finely grated rind of 3 oranges
45ml/3 tbsp golden (light corn) syrup
10ml/2 tsp vanilla extract
icing (confectioners') sugar, for dusting

> **COOK'S TIP**
> Baking time is important with these biscuits: cook them for too long and they scorch, but if you take them out too early they won't be crisp, so keep a close eye on them in the last few minutes of baking.

Per 2 cookies: Gluten free; Energy 352kcal/1467kJ; Protein 4g; Carbohydrate 37g, of which sugars 22g; Fat 22g, of which saturates 14g; Cholesterol 53mg; Calcium 32mg; Fibre 1g; Sodium 168mg.

Preheat the oven to 190°C/375°F/Gas 5. Line two large baking sheets with baking parchment.

With an electric mixer or a wooden spoon, beat the butter and sugar together until light and fluffy.

Stir in the quinoa flakes and flour with the orange rind, golden syrup and vanilla extract and combine thoroughly.

Place large teaspoonfuls of the mixture on the baking sheets, slightly flattening each one with the back of a damp spoon and leaving a little space for them to spread. Bake for 12–15 minutes, until golden.

Remove from the oven and leave on the baking trays for 5 minutes, then transfer to a wire rack to cool. Dust with icing sugar and serve.

DATE AND WALNUT QUINOA FLAPJACKS

This recipe is a tasty and effective twist on traditional flapjacks. It uses quinoa flakes, which are more substantial than rolled oats, but still have a delicious gooey sweetness when cooked.

Makes 8

115g/4oz/½ cup butter
75g/3oz/6 tbsp muscovado (molasses) sugar
30ml/2 tbsp golden (light corn) syrup
50g/2oz/⅓ cup dates, finely chopped
30ml/2 tbsp roughly chopped walnuts
115g/4oz/1 cup quinoa flakes
30ml/2 tbsp rolled oats
5ml/1 tsp mixed (apple pie) spice

VARIATION
Replace the golden (light corn) syrup with honey, and use alternative fruit and nuts if you prefer

Gluten free; Energy 255kcal/1064kJ; Protein 3g; Carbohydrate 26g, of which sugars 15g; Fat 16g, of which saturates 8g; Cholesterol 30mg; Calcium 35mg; Fibre 2g; Sodium 103mg.

Preheat the oven to 200°C/400°F/Gas 6. Grease and line a 18 x 18cm/ 7 x 7in square baking tin (pan).

In a medium pan, melt the butter, sugar and golden syrup together until the butter has melted; stir to combine. Add the remaining ingredients to the pan and stir well.

Transfer the mixture into the base of the prepared tin, flattening with the back of a wooden spoon and pushing to the edges of the tin until the top is level.

Bake for 12–14 minutes until firm and golden. Score into eight slices while still warm, then leave to cool in the tin until completely cold.

Turn the flapjacks out of the tin. Serve with frothy coffee or hot chocolate. Store in an airtight container.

FLAXSEED AND RAISIN QUINOA MUFFINS

Muffins are great for feeding hungry mouths at the end of the day, or between meals when a high-sugar snack would not give you the same lasting sustenance.

Makes 12

250ml/8fl oz/1 cup buttermilk
150ml/10 fl oz/²⁄₃ cup
*   vegetable oil*
2 eggs
175g/6oz/1½ cups quinoa flour
115g/4oz/1 cup ground
*   flaxseeds (linseeds)*
5ml/1 tsp baking powder
5ml/1 tsp ground cinnamon
5ml/1 tsp ground nutmeg
115g/4oz/²⁄₃ cup caster
*   (superfine) sugar*
50g/2oz/¹⁄₃ cup raisins
30ml/2 tbsp whole flaxseeds,
*   for sprinkling*

Preheat the oven to 200°C/400°F/Gas 6. Pour the buttermilk into a bowl, and beat in the oil and eggs.

Sift the quinoa flour into a large bowl, then stir in the ground flaxseeds, baking powder, ground cinnamon, nutmeg, sugar and raisins.

Make a well in the centre of the dry ingredients, then pour in the buttermilk and egg mixture, stirring briefly to just combine the ingredients. The mixture needs to be of a dropping consistency to ensure a soft crumb, so add a little extra buttermilk if required.

Divide the muffin mixture between 12 muffin tins (pans), lined with paper cases if you wish.

Sprinkle the top of each muffin with a few whole flaxseeds, and use the end of a teaspoon to push any exposed raisins into the batter if you want to avoid any scorching as they cook.

Bake for 18–20 minutes, until the muffins are well risen and firm to the touch. Remove from the tins and cool on a wire rack.

Gluten free; Energy 287kcal/1197kJ; Protein 6g; Carbohydrate 25g, of which sugars 14g; Fat 19g, of which saturates 3g; Cholesterol 23mg; Calcium 51mg; Fibre 2g; Sodium 24mg.

INDEX

bean creole quinoa jambalaya 48
biscuits
   breakfast bars 24
   date and walnut quinoa
     flapjacks 61
   orange quinoa cookies 60
black bean burgers, spicy 52
black quinoa 8, 26, 40, 42
bread
   oat and cinnamon breakfast
     rolls 20

carrot cake, frosted 58
cherry compote, quinoa
   pudding with 56
chicken casserole, Moroccan 38
cookies see biscuits

date and walnut quinoa
   flapjacks 61
drinks
   quinoa powershake 24

edamame bean dip with
   parmesan straws 28
egg-fried quinoa with Chinese
   prawns 35

fennel and orange salad,
   toasted grain 32
fish
   Chinese prawns with egg-
     fried quinoa 35
   quinoa-stuffed trout 36
   salmon and quinoa frittata 18

flaxseed and raisin quinoa
   muffins 62

lamb and black quinoa pilaff 42
lemon and raisin pancakes 22

muesli, multigrain quinoa 17
muffins, flaxseed and raisin
   quinoa muffins 62
mushroom
   mushroom quinoa risotto 45
   shiitake mushroom and
     sesame salad 30

oat and cinnamon breakfast
   rolls 20
orange quinoa cookies 60

pancakes
   lemon and raisin 22
pangrattato
   rocket quinoa pasta with
     pangrattato 49
parmesan straws 28
pasta
   rocket quinoa pasta with
     pangrattato 49
pear and hazelnut crumble 55
pearl quinoa 8, 28, 35, 36, 38, 40,
   46, 48, 49, 50, 52, 56
pork and apple patties, five-
   spiced 40

quinoa
   cooking with 12

health properties of 10
   storing 12
   types of 8
quinoa flakes 9 17, 20, 24, 28, 55,
   60, 61
quinoa flour 9, 22, 40, 52, 55,
   58, 60, 62
quinoa pasta 9, 49
quinoa pops 9, 17, 24
quinoa powershake 24
quinoa pudding with cherry
   compote 56
quinoa sprouts 9
quinoa-stuffed trout 36

red quinoa 8, 18, 32, 40, 45

salad
   shiitake mushroom and
     sesame salad 30
   toasted grain, fennel and
     orange salad 32
salmon and quinoa frittata 18
soup
   fresh tomato and black
     quinoa soup 26

tofu
   Malaysian tofu and quinoa
     laksa 46
tricolour quinoa 8, 30
trout, quinoa-stuffed 36

vegetables with a quinoa and
   cheese crust 50

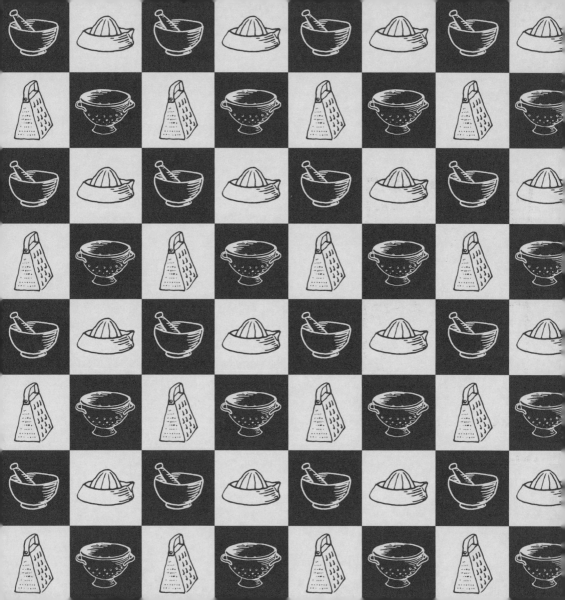